Cheers

Marcia & David Kaplan
Art by Phil Mendez

*The material in this book has
been compiled over a long period
of time. Many of the sources are
unknown to the compilers. We wish
to acknowledge the original
authors whoever they may be.*

*This book is dedicated
to YOU—
the greatest show on earth.*

A smile is contagious—
Let's start
an epidemic.

I have always
known that at
last I would
take this road—
but I did not
know yesterday
that it would
be today.

...K. Rexroth

*If you don't
scale the mountain
you won't see the
view.*

Life is
only what you
make it.
So
make
it
beautiful.

*The only time
you can't
afford to fail
is the last
time you try.*

...Charles Kettering

The harder
we try,
the
luckier we
are.

You have no liabilities—only some assets more developed than others.

The Real Measure

You can use most any
measure when you're speaking
of success.
  You can measure it in a
fancy home, expensive car
or dress.
  But the measure of
your real success is one
you cannot spend —
  It's the way your child
describes you when talking
to a friend.
  ...Martin Baxbaum

He didn't know it couldn't be done, so he went ahead and did it.

No matter what may be your lot in life, build something on it.

The person who
gets
ahead
is the
one who
does more
than
necessary—
and
keeps
on doing it.

*Be someone
who finds
something good
in each day. . .
Then give it
to others.*

Be The Best At Whatever You Are.

If you can't be a pine
  on the top of the hill,
Be a shrub in the valley—
  but be the best little shrub
  this side of the hill;
Be a bush if you cannot be
  a tree.
If you can't be a bush,
  be a bit of the grass—
  some highway happier make;
If you can't be a muskie,
  then just be a bass,
  but the liveliest bass
  in the lake.

We can't all be captains,
  we've got to be crew,
There's something for all
  of us here,
There's big work to do,
  and there's lesser to do,
  and the task we must do is
  the near.
If you can't be a highway
  then just be a trail,
If you can't be the sun,
  be a star;
It isn't by size that you
  win or you fail—
Be the best at whatever
  you are!

                    Douglas Mallcoh

*When you're down
and out, something
always turns up—
if only
your toes.*

*One who fears
failure limits
his worth.*

*Failure is the
opportunity to
begin again more
intelligently.*

...*Henry Ford*

*Happiness is
not a goal,
it is a
by-product.*

...Eleanor Roosevelt

Hitch your wagon to a star.

... *Emerson*

Happy is the person who can laugh at himself.

He will never cease to be amused.

*It's a funny
thing about life:*

*If you refuse
to accept anything
but the very best
you will very
often get it.*

...W. Somerset Maugham

Be what
you wish others
to become.

The opera ain't over till the fat lady sings.

Winners vs. Losers

The Winner—
   is always part of the answer;
The Loser—
   is always part of the problem;
The Winner—
   always has a program;
The Loser—
   always has an excuse;
The Winner—
   says "Let me do it for you;"
The Loser—
   says "That's not my job;"
The Winner—
   sees an answer for every
   problem;
The Loser—
   sees a problem for every
   answer;

The Winner—
    sees a green near every sand
    trap;
The Loser—
    sees two or three sand traps
    near every green;
The Winner—
    says, "It may be difficult
    but it's possible;"
The Loser—
    says, "It may be possible
    but it's too difficult."

BE A WINNER!

You must learn day by day, year by year, to broaden your horizon.

The more things you love, the more you are interested in, the more you enjoy, the more you are indignant about—the more you have left when anything happens.

...Ethel Barrymore

Training that brings about
no change is as effective as
a parachute that opens
on the first bounce.

You may be on the right track ...but you'll get run over if you just sit still.

The really happy man is the one who can enjoy the scenery when he has to take a detour.

*Prevent a
hassle . . .
Smile
first!*

*I believe we are given life
to enjoy and make it more
enjoyable for others.*

*The best way to do
this is to get in the
middle of it.*

...Henry L. Harrell, Sr.

*If you want something
badly enough, you can't
just take it.*

*You have to let it go
free and if it comes back
it's really yours.*

*And if it doesn't—
Well, then you never
really had it anyway!*

Learn from the mistakes of others — you can't live long enough to make them all yourself.

We cannot direct the wind... But we can adjust our sails.

May the very best day of your past be the worst day of your future.

When he took the
job labeled responsible,
  He thought he had
gotten the breaks;
  He wasn't aware
that it meant he'd be
  Responsible for all
mistakes.

...George O. Ludcke

People rarely succeed at anything

unless they have fun doing it.

Earth's great treasure lies in human personality.

...from the Jaycee Creed

The world is a looking glass and gives back to each person a reflection of his attitude.

Don't look back, something might be gaining on you!

... Satchel Paige

Life's greatest thrill is . . . Tomorrow.

. . . Russell De Young

It's not the lions and tigers that'll get you... It's the Mosquitoes!

...*Spurgeon Richardson*

A turtle
only moves ahead
by sticking out
its neck.

Success comes to those who are success conscious.

Failure comes to those who are failure conscious.

Success is just a matter of luck; ask any failure!

If you are
going to walk
on thin ice,
　　You may as
well DANCE.

*It is not I
who speaks,
but Life
within me
who has
much to say.*

Nothing is all wrong.

Even a broken clock is right twice a day.

*Whenever you are
asked if you can do
a job, tell 'em,
   "Certainly I can!"
Then get busy and
find out how to do it.*

. . . *Theodore Roosevelt*

Cooperation is doing with a smile what you have to do anyway.

The great man is he who does not lose his child's heart.

...*Mencius*

He who hesitates is interrupted.

*Don't worry
whether or not the
sun will rise;
	Be prepared to
enjoy it.*

The optimist
fell ten stories.
At each window
he shouted to his
friends:
"All right so far."

Real leaders are ordinary people with extraordinary determination.

*The first step
toward solving
a problem is to
begin.*

Success, like beauty, in all things is individual.

There's only one way to coast — DOWNHILL!

Remember
sugar in coffee
isn't sweet
unless you
stir it up.

Make a lot of
noise, but know
when to fly in
formation.

Happiness is not a destination. It is a way of traveling.

A bird doesn't sing
because it has an answer,
it sings
because it has a song.

...Anglund

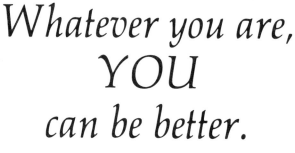

Whatever you are,
YOU
can be better.

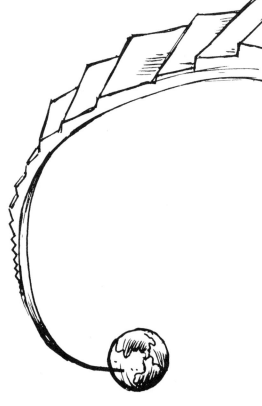

The architect
of the universe didn't
build a stairway
leading nowhere.
Make your time
here an exciting
adventure!

May the dreams of your past be the reality of your future.

We write our own destiny ... We become what we do.

...*Madame Chiang Kai-Shek*

Life is too short to be little...

If better is possible, Good is not enough.

Try, try, try —
Do, do, do —
Now, now,
now!

*It's not
what you know
when you start.
It's what you
learn and put to
good use.*

*You never get
a second chance
to make a
good first
impression.*

You will do
foolish things,
but do them
with enthusiasm.

... *Colette*

The speed of the leader determines the rate of the pack.

Both tears and sweat are salty and wet, but they render different results.

Tears will get you sympathy, but sweat will get you progress.

Winners expect to win in advance.

Life is a self-fulfilling prophecy.

HIGH JUMP

The Past: It is
history.
   Make the
present good and
the past will
take care of
itself.

We are continually
faced by great
opportunities
brilliantly disguised
as insoluble problems.

*Dedication is
more important than
ability,
   But when you have
both . . .
   Success is all
yours.*

   . . . Art Neiman

*Every job is a
self-portrait of
the person who
did it.
Autograph your
work with
excellence.*

Love doesn't make the world go round. Love is what makes the ride worthwhile.

...*Franklin P. Jones*

There is no
limit to what can
be done—
　　If it doesn't
matter who gets the
credit.

The purpose of life is not to be happy. It is to matter, to be productive, to make some difference you lived at all.

. . . Leo Rosten

*Your luck
is how
you treat
people.*

Act as though it were impossible to fail.

Maturity is the ability to live in peace with that which we cannot change.

. . .*Ann Landers*

Winning isn't everything— Wanting to is!

...*Arnold Palmer*

The best preparation for tomorrow is to give life my best Today!

May you
LIVE
all the days
of your life.

Cheers to You!

USE THIS CONVENIENT ORDER FORM FOR ADDITIONAL
COPIES OF ALL THE KAPLAN BOOKS

NAME _____

ADDRESS _____

CITY _____

STATE _____ ZIP CODE _____

I WOULD LIKE TO ORDER:

_____ CHEERS BOOKS @ $5.95

_____ SMILES BOOKS @ $5.95

_____ FRIENDS BOOKS @ $5.95

_____ HAPPINESS BOOKS @ $5.95

_____ THANKS BOOKS @ $5.95

_____ 3 BOOK SETS WITH SLIP COVER @ $17.50
(CHEERS, SMILES, FRIENDS)

PLEASE SEND ORDER FORM AND CHECK OR MONEY ORDER
TO: **CHEERS, P.O. BOX 550513, ATLANTA, GA. 30355-3013**

USE THIS CONVENIENT ORDER FORM FOR ADDITIONAL
COPIES OF ALL THE KAPLAN BOOKS

NAME _____

ADDRESS _____

CITY _____

STATE _____ ZIP CODE _____

I WOULD LIKE TO ORDER:

_____ CHEERS BOOKS @ $5.95

_____ SMILES BOOKS @ $5.95

_____ FRIENDS BOOKS @ $5.95

_____ HAPPINESS BOOKS @ $5.95

_____ THANKS BOOKS @ $5.95

_____ 3 BOOK SETS WITH SLIP COVER @ $17.50
(CHEERS, SMILES, FRIENDS)

PLEASE SEND ORDER FORM AND CHECK OR MONEY ORDER
TO: **CHEERS, P.O. BOX 550513, ATLANTA, GA. 30355-3013**